The Rise And Fall Of The Sewing Machine Kings
by
Alex Askaroff

The Rise And Fall Of The Sewing Machine Kings
By
Alex I Askaroff

This is no masterpiece. It's more a self-published labour of love from someone who has spent a lifetime in the sewing trade and a million hours gathering facts for you. From my vast profits of around 10p a book I'll retire to my beach hut and fish all day. Why write it? Well no one else bothers! Please forgive my spelling, United Kingdom English, and enjoy it in the spirit it was written. Also I found it impossible to split into chapters. Just go with the flow.

The first sewing machine with some very useful ideas was patented by Elias Howe in 1846. He was the son of an American farmer from Spencer, Massachusetts and had learnt his trade working in the textile mills of Lowell. There were lots of machines before his but none really worked that well.

Today many countries claim it was one of their sons that invented the humble domestic appliance but it was America where it all really happened. Until the computer took its crown, for over a century, the humble sewing machine was the most mass produced item to be used for industrial and domestic purposes in the world.

However before the industry really got off the ground there was a huge problem, one that would stifle not only competition but the birth of true mass production. During the 1850's sewing machine manufacture was crippled by a handful of powerful men. Production of the world's first mass-produced sewing machines was constantly being stopped by court cases brought about by men who became known at the time as the Sewing Machine Kings. These men were engaged in the Great Sewing Machine Wars.

Money was being lost in time-wasting litigation and the evolution of the humble sewing machine, hailed as the most useful invention of the 19th Century, almost ground to a halt. The largest litigation in American court history was taking place, and splashed across the publications of the day.

Elias Howe went from being a poor farmer's son to one of the richest men of his age. Unfortunately all the money in the world could not buy him good health!

The main instigator of the litigation was our farmer's son Elias Howe, who was furious at everyone making sewing machines except him. He was closely followed by Isaac Merritt Singer. Although Isaac was never credited with any major sewing machine invention, in 1851 he did put together the first really good sewing machine and was sneaky enough to buy up any patents available to protect his market. His sewing machine was the first machine that did what it said on the tin. It was reasonably easy to use and even came with a guarantee. The only fly in the ointment was that he had used all the best ideas around and ended up in court.

Isaac Merritt Singer was by far the most flamboyant of all the Sewing Machine Kings. His early years as an actor was the perfect grounding for the showman and inventor. Although Isaac was never credited with any crucial sewing machine patents, what he did was far more important. He built the first ever decent sewing machine (by copying others) that allowed all others makers to prosper in his wake. Singer led one of the most extraordinary rags-to-riches life and for a time lived the American Dream.

The main stranglehold of the industry came about because Elias Howe had patented the first lock-stitch shuttle machine with a steel shuttle and needle with an eye at the bottom-end (they were all at the top before that). In reality his patent machine never worked particularly well and in all his years he made less than six machines. However he did hold those two essential patents, and from 1846, it crippled almost every other sewing machine manufacturer.

Here is one of only a handful of genuine Elias Howe 'hand built machines'. Elias would spend ages painstakingly building each machine and they are works of art. This one is in the Science Museum, London, England. Although Elias made a fortune from his sewing machine patents, he built less than six machines!

Howe had not invented the first sewing machine but he had patents and patents could be protected. His fanciful meandering reasons of how he came about one of his inventions are pretty far-fetched.

His idea of the needle with the point at the bottom end apparently came to him after a dream. Native Indians were shooting arrows and one flew through a wigwam, the point pulling a thread with it. It may be true. Or possibly he had seen a British patent with a similar needle.

The most likely scenario is that he had seen the multiple sewing machines that had been around for years and although they were pretty useless, he managed to pick up the essentials from them. He may even have seen Walter Hunt's machine that had been on public display many years earlier. What Elias's did, which was genius, was to create a metal shuttle, basically a tiny version of the large wooden loom shuttles he had been fixing during his time in the textile mills.

This allowed his machine to catch a single thread travelling vertically, with one travelling horizontally (the warp and the weave) creating a lock stitch. This lock stitch allowed us for the first time to properly join two pieces of material together. Elias's machine could repeat this 'locking stitch' 500 times every minute (so he said, no one else seemed to be able to manage it). At the time it was like magic and apparently shows were set up to demonstrate this amazing ability on Broadway, New York. For 10 cents a time you could see two pieces of fabric joined by 'a sewing engine'. The future was here. But we still had the problem of patent protection stopping any other companies making sewing machines.

In the constant court battles between the patent holders and the people trying to break them, Walter Hunt, backed by Isaac Singer, produced conclusive evidence of the sewing machine that he had invented long before Elias Howe's.

Isaac Singer had tried on many occasions to break Howe's patents, this time reproducing Hunt's earlier sewing machine that he had made in his basement in 1834, (using a similar needle and shuttle to Howe's machine). It was all very drawn out and utterly confusing but it did the daily periodicals some great press. At one point a fight even broke out between the enormous six foot five Singer and the diminutive Elias Howe. Isaac had gambled everything on beating Howe, giving away half his company to his legal partner Edward Clark in return for his services.

In the end all Singer's efforts did not matter. The courts took the basic fact that Hunt never patented his machine before putting it on public display as the deciding factor. He may have invented an earlier machine but in the eyes of the law it was not protected.

So why did Walter never patent such a valuable item? Walter Hunt was a prolific inventor, he even invented the safety pin. Some say that he never patented his sewing machine because his daughter who was worried that having a machine do the work of several women would lead to a collapse in their industry causing even more poverty amongst the low paid workers of America. As it turned out the sewing machine led to one of the largest expansion of industry ever seen and cheaper clothes for one and all. His story is a fascinating tale especially where he ended up being buried. You can read more about him in my other publication, Walter Hunt the man who really invented the sewing machine on Amazon.

Hunt and Singer lost their case and Howe walked out of court triumphant with his basic ideas protected. The Great Sewing Machine Wars thundered on.

Right or wrong Howe continued suing anyone who dared make a sewing machine without paying him royalties. From then on the skittles fell quickly and Howe won his cases, one after another. He became the all-powerful litigator. Howe not only sued anyone who made sewing machines but also people who bought them. He did it very publicly, advertising his wins in the papers to scare away potential sewing machine customers.

Allen B Wilson was a prolific inventor and spent a huge amount of his time trying to get around Elias Howe's patents by designing different methods to form a stitch. His 'four motion feed' is still used on most sewing machines to this day.

Isaac Singer was busily doing the same. Then we throw two more powerhouses into the pot. One was Allen B. Wilson and his partner Nathaniel Wheeler. They were running the largest sewing machine company in America at the time. Wilson had invented and patented two brilliant ideas, the rotary hook, (which got around Howe's shuttle patent) and the four-motion feed, which still moves the work on most sewing machines today.

Wheeler & Wilson sewing machines were superbly engineered but with mass production speeding up they became out priced. People could buy a sewing machine for less than a quarter of the one above. They are highly prized today.

The other powerhouse at the time was The Grover & Baker Sewing Machine Company. They produced the finest machines on the market using a looper instead of Howe's shuttle and two reels of thread, one on top and one below the machine (why has no one ever copied that!). William O. Grover and William Emerson Baker were two Boston tailors. William Grover was fascinated by the early sewing machines and being a tailor knew what benefit a good sewing machine would make to his industry. During the 1840's Grover continually experimented with sewing machines, concentrating on the lower thread mechanism and by May 8th 1849 was granted his first patent.

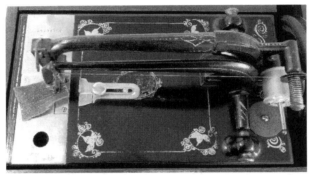

Grover & Baker made the most expensive machines. Superbly built and finished (some in mother of pearl). They also used the brilliant idea of two reels of thread. This machine has a cotton reel on top of the machine and another underneath. No bobbins to worry about! Like some other manufacturers their prices continued to rise as others fell. This proved disastrous for the pioneers and they soon faded from history.

Let's step back a moment and sum up this complex situation. In 1855 the big sewing machine companies, Singer, Howe, Grover & Baker and Wheeler & Wilson, own a whole pocket full of patents. A sewing machine was near impossible to make or sell without them. So what were these

Sewing Machine Kings all doing instead of becoming rich manufacturing a product that every household wanted? They were spending most of their days in court suing each other. The silly boys.

The only people making any real money were the lawyers. Something had to be done, step forward, Orlando. B. Potter. He was the lawyer for Grover & Baker Sewing Machines. Orlando was a peacemaker, the Henry Kissinger of his time. He could stand back from the fight and see the solution that would make all the parties unite with one common interest, profit. Orlando saw first-hand all the litigation papers. His office had over 700,000 pieces of legal paper alone. Like several of the sewing machine makers they had to have a special library built to house them all.

Orlando Potter came up with a very cunning plan that would make a handful of men filthy rich (though publicly detested). All he had to do was get all the parties around a table without killing each other and explain his idea. The plan was simple and deadly, to pool or combine all the main patents into one pot. In one foul swoop a few men would control almost the entire sewing machine industry in America.

After much talking and promises of untold wealth a final meeting took place on 24th October 1856 in Albany, New York. All the main characters signed a peace pact. The Sewing Machine Kings, agreed to pool their nine 'all-important' patents and form a Cartel or Combination. The Albany Agreement was the first 'patent pool' in American history and brought to an end the Great Sewing Machine Wars.

And so in 1856 the Sewing Machine Combination was formed. Now these Sewing Machine Kings could mercilessly pounce on any small company who dared to step out of line, trying to make a sewing machine without paying the big boys. Many small companies folded under the pressure. Some, like Charles Raymond, escaped and built his machines over the border in Canada where he was not under their yoke. All the rest had to pay royalties to the Combination or fold.

These sewing machines became known as New England machines as they were made in that area around the time of The American Civil War. However with the Sewing Machine Combination manipulating sewing machine manufacturing, many businesses closed and some, like Raymond, fled to Canada, free from so many patent restrictions,

opening a successful sewing machine company in Guelph, Ontario.

The Sewing Machine Combination became an all-powerful monopoly and pretty illegal really. A loop-hole in the law allowed the Combination to continue even though the public hated it. It also crippled mass expansion in the sewing trade.

The Sewing Machine Combination was attacked in the courts but it held firm. Every sewing machine made by any company in America had to pay the combination $15 per sewing machine manufactured. That is the equivalent of several weeks' wages today. The money was split between the Singer Company, Howe, Grover & Baker and Wheeler & Wilson. Elias Howe taking the lion's share of $5 per machine, because he held those two dubious but all-important patents.

Cleverly all the Kings put $3 of their takings into a fighting fund, a pot to sue any company that tried to make a sewing machine without paying. Like my mum always said, "Remember the golden rule. The one with the gold makes the rule!" The stranglehold that the Sewing Machine Combination held over America was total.

To recap a handful of powerful men in America held all the essential patents for sewing machines, making it impossible for any manufacturer to make a sewing machine without paying the Sewing Machine Combination a fee. The handful of men in the Combination grew in wealth as they controlled the production of sewing machines throughout America.

It was not all bad news. Though the monopoly was unfair it allowed all the sewing machine makers to get on with, guess what! Sewing machines. From the 1860's, for the first time in history, we see sewing machines flourish. Staggeringly Elias Howe, who had made a fortune from his licensing fees, somehow managed to get his patents extended in 1860, claiming that he had not received a reasonable recompense for his inventions!

Willcox & Gibbs continued to flourish in the sewing machine business, finally closing in the 1990's. This chainstitch machine was capable of sewing at 4,000 stitches a minute and was almost silent in operation.

Firms like Willcox & Gibbs could now manufacture machines for the masses. They paid their licence fees and made their stunning machines. Their silent chain stitch was so successful that it hardly changed for nearly 70 years. They were used by everyone from the lady in the parlour to the hats factories as they could also fly along at over 4,000 stitches a minute, something that very few machines can even do today. By 1870 the factory in Providence, Rhode Island, producing Willcox & Gibbs models was making around 15,000 hand-built sewing machines a year.

The years from the mid 1850's to the 1870's were the glory years for the Sewing Machine Kings. However, like a house of cards, eventually it all came crashing down.

Firstly the patents started running out and then Congress managed to shut the loop-hole in the law that was allowing the Sewing Machine Combination's illegal monopoly. Even Wilson failed to have his patent extended in 1877. Secondly, several of the Sewing machine Kings started dying off.

You might be wondering what happened to those powerful men who held such control over America. Walter Hunt (who was not part of the Combination but an integral part of our story), died of pneumonia aged 63 in June of 1859, after falling ill in his workshop, still inventing. Elias Howe, the poor farmer's son went on to become one of the richest men in America, earning over $2,000,000 in licence fees alone (before losing most of it and dying at the tender age of 48 in 1867). Though in life the men detested one another they are both interred at Green Wood Cemetery in New York, just a hop away from each other.

Isaac was not far behind in wealth but he was a man of passion. You will just have to read his story, the naughty boy. He had so many wives, mistresses, and children that after his death his will was not sorted out for several years, mainly because more and more kids claimed he was their father. In the end at least 20 of his children were left part of the amazing Singer fortune.

Isaac Singer was an extraordinary and complicated man. He grew from a penniless cunning and devious street-wise kid, living on his wits, to one of the richest men in the world. His character also changed from cold-blooded and ruthless in his youth, to a cheerful old benefactor throwing children's parties in his old age.

When Isaac Singer died, aged 63 in 1875, the public read the papers in disbelief, with open-mouths and with bulging eyes. How could it be possible that one man who had come from nothing, almost begging on the streets, die one of the richest men on the planet?

In his later, years rich old Singer, had married a half French model 30 years his junior (sounds so familiar). You may have seen the beautiful Isabella Eugenie Boyer without realizing it as many say she modelled for The Statue of Liberty.

Isaac died in his own partially finished palace in Paignton, England, probably with a smile on his face! Today his wonderful palace is closed to the public and slowly perishes due to council neglect.

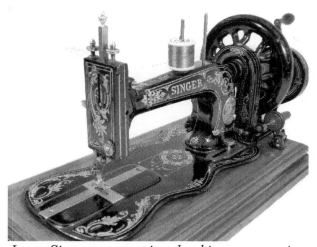

Isaac Singer was not involved in many sewing machines but he was still getting royalties from the Singer Company until his death. The model 12 became the bestselling sewing machine of the 19th Century running from 1865 right up to 1900. The Singer name was first put across the arm after the opening of the Kilbowie Factory in Scotland in 1883.

Aged 47, Allen B Wilson, had taken the opportunity to remove himself from the battlefield of the sewing machine industry on grounds of ill health. In 1870 his worth was considerable, he had a personal estate of $130,000 plus another $150,000 in land. This represents over $100,000,000 today. Wilson died in 1888 and Nathaniel Wheeler five years later in 1893.

Our peacemaker, Orlando Brunson Potter, went on to run Grover & Baker and much more. The superb legal mind and businessman (who had managed to get all the Sewing Machine Kings together without killing each other) became a member of the United

States House of Representatives. He worked tirelessly to establish the National Banking Act in the U S and died one of the wealthiest men in New York City in January 1894.

Edward Cabot Clark, the man who fought Singer's battles in court and who owned half of Singer's business empire went on to build the Dakota Buildings in New York City where John Lennon was shot dead. Clark died in 1882. It is said he still haunts the building.

So that was that! Today no more than a footnote in history. However, let's step back a second and wrap up this story by looking at what happened when the Sewing Machine cartel and the Sewing Machine Kings were finally ousted.

In 1877, for the first time, all the sewing machine makers were free from royalty payments and patent infringements on all the main features of sewing machines. This led to the first real sewing machine boom. True mass production of the most wanted modern marvel flourished, providing millions of jobs around the world. Britain, France, Germany and many more countries jumped on the bandwagon making countless millions of sewing machines each year.

*Once most of the patents had expired sewing
machine makers flourished like this Gresham made
in England in the 1880's.*

Mass production also meant the price of sewing machines fell dramatically and many different styles appeared. New methods for buying sewing machines also helped. Edward Clark had instigated the first ever properly organized hire purchase, layaway or instalment plan scheme. People thought he was crazy to give away a sewing machine and trust the public to pay for it over several years. However he proved them all wrong, the public could be trusted and sewing machine manufacture went through the roof. From then on most other businesses, in all fields, started to offer hire purchase on any expensive item.

The French always used inspiring designs in their sewing machines. The Incomparable also had a walking foot and was operated by a simple pulley mechanism.

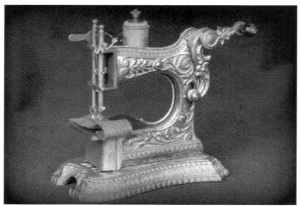

The Germans came up with some stunning models. This is the Muller model 6 and would have only been bought by the wealthiest families as a child's toy. It produced a simple chainstitch.

In their heyday Wheeler & Wilson had initially stormed ahead. However the Singer Company just kept on growing. It caught up Wheeler & Wilson, bought them out, used the Bridgeport factories and flew on. For nearly 100 years no other sewing machine company came close to Singer.

By 1890 the Singer Corporation, through ruthless advertising, brilliant market management, aggressive expansion, superb engineering and quality products dominated world trade in sewing machines, producing nearly 75% of all sales.

It is said that the sewing machine industries modern manufacturing techniques combined with their state of the art supply and demand, from railways to ports, helped to kick start the greatest industrial growth that America had ever seen and helped to make it into the world's first super power.

All this is ancient history now. Today we take for granted the humble little sewing machine that still touches all our daily lives. However many years ago those machines exploded onto the market with the impact of a nuclear bomb and for nearly two decades they were ruled over by a handful of powerful men, once known as the Sewing Machine Kings.

The End

The Rise And Fall Of The Sewing Machine Kings
by
Alex Askaroff

To see Alex Askaroff's work
Visit Amazon
www.sewalot.com

Isaac Singer
The First capitalist

No1 New Release Amazon 2014. Most of us know the name Singer but few are aware of his amazing life story, his rags to riches journey from a little runaway to one of the richest men of his age. The story of Isaac Merritt Singer will blow your mind, his wives and lovers, castles and palaces.

No1 New Release. No1 Bestseller
Amazon certified.

*If this isn't the perfect book it's
close to it!
I'm on my third run though
already.
Love it, love it, love it.
F. Watson USA*

Elias Howe
The Man Who Changed The World
No1 New Release Amazon Oct 2019.

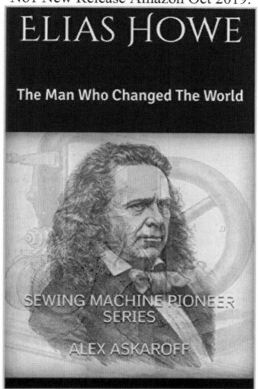

Anyone who uses a sewing machine today has one person to thank, Elias Howe. He was the young farmer with a weak body who figured it out. Elias's life was short and hard, from the largest court cases in legal history to his adventures in the American Civil War. He carved out a name that will live forever. Elias was 48 when he died. In that short time he really was the man who changed the world.

Printed in Great Britain
by Amazon